MEDICAL MALPRACTICE
&
OTHER LAWSUITS:

A HEALTHCARE
PROVIDER'S GUIDE

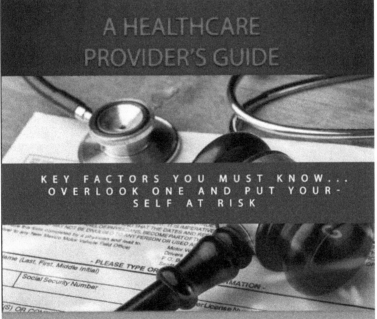

KEY FACTORS YOU MUST KNOW...
OVERLOOK ONE AND PUT YOUR-
SELF AT RISK

For More Resources:

http://www.MedLawCompliance.com

Legal and Copyright

Copyright ©2017 MedLawCompliance.com
All rights reserved. No part of this publication may be reproduced, distributed, or transmitted in any form or by any means, including photocopying, recording, or other electronic or mechanical methods, without the prior written permission of the publisher, except in the case of brief quotations embodied in critical reviews and certain other noncommercial uses permitted by copyright law.

Published by: The Obvious Authority
1235 Upper Front Street #285
Binghamton, NY 13905
support@obviousauthority.com

Disclaimer:
Nothing contained in this book is to be considered as the rendering of legal advice to the reader. Readers are responsible for determining the applicable law and for obtaining legal advice from their own health care attorneys.

Most of the topics discussed in this book are dependent either on the laws of a particular state or on federal legislation. Because both federal and state laws change continually, you should not rely on any particular section of the book as being the law of the state in which you practice at any particular time.

Nothing contained in this book is intended to establish a standard of care in any medical discipline or specialty. This book should not be considered to establish a standard of care, and the contents of this book should not be cited in support of any particular practice or procedure. Further, the suggestions in this book do not necessarily reflect the opinions of the author.

Finally, the author does not endorse any particular product or vendor.

Ordering Information:
Quantity sales. Special discounts are available on quantity purchases by corporations, associations, and others. For details, contact the publisher at the address above.

Printed in the United States of America
First Edition

Table of Contents

Introduction & Overview

In 1923, Dr. Donald Gregg published an article in the
Boston Medical and Surgical Journal, subsequently
renamed the New England Journal of Medicine in 1928,
discussing the art and science of medicine due to the
growing concern that the "art" of medicine would be
supplanted by the "science" of medicine. Although the
practice of medicine is clearly anchored in strong scientific
roots, the art of practicing medicine remains important for
patient care delivery, despite the dramatic ongoing shifts in
our healthcare system. As we are not dealing with an exact
science, the risk of a medical malpractice or other lawsuit
looms over all healthcare providers – physicians, nurse
practitioners, physician assistants, general and specialist
nurses, therapists, et cetera.

Despite the medical malpractice crises, there has been a
decrease in the number of medical malpractice lawsuits
filed over the past few years. Although seemingly positive
news, the amount of money paid per claim has shown a
steady and significant increase. Medical malpractice claims
can result in excessive malpractice insurance premiums,
inability to obtain insurance, sanctions, severe emotional

stress, and risking personal assets, among other potential devastating problems for the healthcare provider.

Hearing a witness allege that you harmed or even killed your patient is devastating. It is not easy to see that one person as the anomaly and your other 2,000+ patients as the norm. Your view of people and even your job can become jaded.

Some problems arise when unrealistic patient expectations collide with the reality that physicians cannot cure everything. Many medical problems can be helped, but not all can be solved with a pill or surgery. Doctors are human. The world is not perfect. Patients are not all equally educated, good listeners, compliant or even physically and mentally capable of following a doctor's advice.

Both hospitals and health care providers are affected by the rising costs of malpractice insurance. If doctors cannot afford coverage, they end up retiring early, relocating their practices to geographic areas with lower premiums or restricting their practice to less liability-driven practice areas. In turn, hospitals have difficulty finding coverage in certain specialties where the insurance premiums are high.

Money permeates both sides of the doctor-patient relationship. The more the patient spends to seek health care, the greater the expectations. As health care insurance premiums and medication costs rise, health care delivery does not increase proportionately. Patient expectations cannot always be met.

The cost to attend college, much less medical school, is astronomical. It is not unusual for a young physician to owe hundreds of thousands of dollars of student debt. While it is true that physicians take the Hippocratic Oath to help people, they do not take an oath to deliver all health care for free. They need to charge for their time spent delivering health care to the public.

The less the doctor makes per visit, the more patients the doctor has to see to earn the same money. Physicians have to support themselves and their families. They cannot be on call 24/7 without risking bad health themselves. There is always a balancing act. Physicians and other health care professionals work hard and sacrifice a lot to give patients the best health care, advice, and services possible. But hard work and selfless devotion is not enough.

Sometimes it seems that patients expect the moon and stars, all delivered on a silver platter. Their health insurance companies promise them they will receive the highest quality all of the time, while frequently creating road blocks to your recommendations and prescriptions to save money. While the doctors try to deliver high quality care, it is impossible for every patient to be diagnosed and cured immediately during the first examination.

In addition, patients have to share the burden of their good health. They need to listen to the advice given, get the medical testing that has been ordered, take their medications faithfully and return for follow-up visits regularly as scheduled. Quality medical care is a two-way street, with both the health care providers and the patient consumers sharing responsibility for obtaining the end goal – good health.

When you couple unrealistic expectations with today's Internet world, the crisis escalates. After all, patients come to you with their extensive medical knowledge, all found on the Internet, where they can learn how to diagnose themselves after watching and listening to a You Tube. If the heath care provider dares to disagree with their personal medical diagnosis, a disagreement easily ensues.

Further causing antagonism is the cost of health care insurance premiums. The more you pay, the higher the expectation that the diagnosis and prognosis will be made quickly and correctly. The increased copays associated with medical testing does not help the situation. After all, the patient who has diagnosed himself/herself via the Internet does not really need the expensive testing. Add to that the high cost of pharmaceuticals – paying for medications is often prohibitive.

EMR has made the doctor-patient interactions less personal. For every 15-minute visit, possibly 3 minutes or less of it is spent actually looking the patient in the eye. Patients do not get to know the doctor. It is much easier to sue someone you do not know than someone you feel is your friend and on your side.

Everyone knows that doctors make too much money. Otherwise, why would Congress and insurance companies need to continually cut their reimbursement? So it does not bother certain patients if the doctor has to part with some of it in a lawsuit. Plus, plaintiff attorneys remind the public all the time that there is "no" malpractice crisis.

This book will serve as a general primer for new and seasoned physicians and other providers in the health care arena. It gives an overview of the types of medical malpractice insurance that is required in most states to practice medicine and ideas on how to avoid lawsuits in medicine. It will make you aware of the types of other lawsuits that can be filed as a result of your practicing medicine and how to avoid them. You will be educated on the defense of a lawsuit and what it entails.

I wrote this based on my over 30 years of experience in practicing medicine full time in Philadelphia, Pennsylvania, teaching an upper level law school course entitled "Current Problems in Law and Medicine" for over 20 years at the Beasley School of Law, Temple University, and being involved in the medical professional liability discipline.

Additionally, I have spoken with innumerable professionals and patients across the United States, serving as a risk management and educational consultant and keynote speaker on medical professional liability, patient safety, risk management, health care compliance, and medical ethics.

This book is meant for general information purposes exclusively. Nothing contained in this book is to be considered as the rendering of legal advice to the readers or establishing a standard of care. Readers are responsible for determining the applicable law and for obtaining legal advice from their own health care attorneys.

Chapter 1: Malpractice Insurance

If you are found to have acted negligently in your practice, patients are able to recover "compensatory damages" for their lost earnings, pain and suffering and medical bills causally related to your negligence. The purpose of professional negligence insurance, commonly known as "medical malpractice insurance," is to provide compensation to a patient for injuries associated with a health care provider's medical negligence.

Choosing a Malpractice Insurance Company

When choosing potential insurers for malpractice coverage, first consider the financial stability of the company. In recent years, many have bankrupted, so the financial status is important. The best place to research the financial stability of a potential malpractice carrier is with the insurance rating agencies, A.M. Best & Co., Fitch Rating, Demotech and Standard & Poor's – these bureaus assess the insurance company's ability to pay future claims. A financial rating of A- or better is preferable.

Cost Factors

Most states mandate that physicians who practice medicine maintain malpractice insurance coverage. Yet the cost of malpractice insurance has escalated over the years. In the 1970s, there was a large increase in the number of lawsuits filed. Then in the 1980s, both the number of lawsuits filed and the amount of money paid out for lawsuits increased. These problems have escalated to the point that premiums have soared in many parts of the country. The cost of medical malpractice insurance coverage over the past 5 to 10 years has fortunately stabilized.

The cost for the medical malpractice insurance coverage depends on a variety of factors, including the geographic area in which you practice, the field of medicine which you practice, whether you perform complicated or risky procedures or surgeries and your past claims history. When buying any insurance, including malpractice insurance, you should "shop" around and get different price quotes if you are in a geographic area where that is feasible. Sometimes you can get a discount in your malpractice policy if you agree to take a Risk Management course.

In addition to checking the financial stability of the company and comparing prices, you need to review the details of the policy.

Types of Medical Malpractice Policies

There are 3 basic types of malpractice policies available:
- The most common policy purchased is a "claims-made" policy. This covers a doctor for medical malpractice claims that are made and incidents that are reported during the policy period. The insurance policy itself specifically lists when the "policy period" begins and ends. The main issue that arises with this type of coverage surrounds what is a "claim." Do you, for example, need to report every patient complaint, no matter how frivolous, to your carrier?
- An "occurrence" policy covers claims that are made or incidents that are reported during the policy period regardless of when the suit is filed or when you report the incident. Occurrence policies are rarely used these days.
- The third type of malpractice insurance is a "claims-paid" policy. These are rarely used because the premiums are based only on claims settled during the previous year and projected for the current year.

The claim is generally not considered made until the actual lawsuit has commenced. This kind of policy can be assessed even after the policy has ended. When changing from a claims-paid policy, the physician usually has to purchase tail coverage from that company, which is quite expensive.

The Problems with the Different Types of Policies

Assume that you, a rational doctor and educated consumer, purchase a claims-made malpractice insurance policy. As indicated above, the policy will state the period during which the claim has to be made to be covered and it will also state when the malpractice had to have occurred in order for your malpractice to be covered. If you retire or change employers, there may be a gap in your insurance coverage for treatment provided before the earliest date the current policy covers. This gap is even wider if you take care of young children or incompetent adults. In both of those cases, the time period in which a lawsuit can be successfully brought against you (i.e., the statute of limitations) is usually extended until after the minor reaches the age of majority (usually 18 years of age) or until after the incompetency ends.

Tail Coverage Fills the Gap

If you retire, tail coverage is used in conjunction with claims-made policies to cover lawsuits brought against you for a set number of years in the future after your last policy has ended. That is, it covers claims that occur because of incidents during the coverage period, even though your coverage has already ended. While this coverage is expensive, it is worth the cost. Without tail coverage, you will not only have to pay for any judgment against you but you will also have to pay for the costs of defense of the lawsuit itself.

Most insurance companies will give you tail coverage automatically for no charge if you become permanently disabled or retire, as long as you have had continuous coverage with a claims-made policy for many years. You can also buy "nose coverage," which covers prior acts. This is very difficult to obtain unless you have had uninterrupted coverage. It is also very expensive.

No matter what type of malpractice coverage you have, a number of other issues must be considered.

When One Carrier Insures You and the Hospital

Do not use the same carrier as the hospital with which you are affiliated uses if you can avoid doing so. If you are both named in a lawsuit, you may be the underdog, since the hospital pays exorbitant malpractice fees and probably has more leverage. If a single law firm defends both you and the hospital, this may result in a serious conflict of interest.

Typical Malpractice Policy Coverage

If there is an allegation that a healthcare provider was negligent, medical malpractice insurance covers the costs associated with defense of the allegation, including expenses, defense attorney fees, court costs and any settlements or judgments. Without malpractice insurance, physicians and healthcare providers would have to pay personally for these expenses, in addition to being held personally liable for any settlements or judgments resulting from a lawsuit.

The typical malpractice policy pays the injured party for "compensatory damages," which are designed to compensate the patient for harm caused by the health care provider's mistake and to make the patient "whole." This includes compensation for lost wages, medical bills, and pain and suffering.

Typical Malpractice Policy Exclusions

Most malpractice policies exclude:

- Payment of punitive damages (awarded to the injured party to punish the healthcare provider for his or her actions). Punitive damages are rarely awarded in medical malpractice cases. They are applicable only if the doctor acted outrageously, by intentionally causing the injury or by disregarding the patient's health to such an extent that the wanton or reckless disregard for the patient shocks the conscience of a reasonable person.

- Intentional acts, criminal conduct, grossly negligent conduct, libel (written falsehoods), and slander (oral falsehoods). Under such circumstances, the healthcare provider has to retain a private attorney to defend such claims. As an example, a hospital nurse sued a primary care osteopathic physician. She was complaining of a sore neck when he was walking past her in the hospital. She claimed he reached out and yanked her neck, causing her severe and debilitating pain and ending her nursing career. He claimed that she asked him to help "fix" her neck pain so he did a routine osteopathic manipulation.

If this conduct had been "proven" to the satisfaction of the jury, the injuries associated with the "intentional" acts of assault and battery (usually defined as intentional unwanted touching) would not have been covered by his malpractice policy because he had no doctor-patient relationship. That is, he could have been held personally responsible for the injuries allegedly associated with his actions. The case was settled out of court.

Consent to Settle

Another issue that arises is the malpractice carrier's ability to settle a case with or without the doctor's consent. It is very likely that under certain circumstances, an insurance company will want to avoid a jury verdict at all costs, even though you are perfectly willing and interested in having the case against you tried in court. If you want to avoid having the carrier settle a case you think should be tried, insist on having a "right to consent" addendum to your policy. This allows you, the doctor whose name will end up in the National Data Bank, to decide if, and on what terms, a case can be settled without a trial.

Indemnifying Insurers

In many health insurance provider contracts, if you want to become a participating doctor in the plan, you have to sign a contract that includes a clause that holds the insurance plan "harmless" if the insurance company is sued because of your malfeasance (bad action) or nonfeasance (lack of action). This is a classic Catch-22 scenario. The plan tells you what to do and you do it, and then you are responsible for all problems that result from doing what you were forced to do.

Your provider contract is very likely to contain language that forces you to pay the judgment rendered against the insurer as well as the insurer's attorney fees and costs to defend the case. Therefore, it is extremely important to carefully review the terms of both your personal malpractice policy and the insurance plan contract insofar as they relate to this issue.

Risk Assessments

Many practices are asking their malpractice insurance companies carriers and/or private risk management companies to conduct malpractice risk assessments. A team of risk managers will come to your office to try to uncover all sources of potential malpractice. They try to determine what you and your staff are doing and not doing that could eventually result in claims against you. They review the way you document charts, handle electronic medical records, make appointments, schedule follow-ups, refer patients and handle other routine procedures that are particular to the way you conduct your office and hospital practice.

Remember patient confidentiality! Do not forget that your patient has a right to privacy in this situation as well as in the traditional doctor-patient contacts. You need to make sure that during this assessment, your patient's privacy is protected. Eradicate all personal information from patient charts that are reviewed, do not disclose patient names, et cetera. Make sure you have a valid Business Associate Agreement in place prior to the risk assessment.

Additional Insurance You May Need

If you are concerned that your regular malpractice policy is not sufficient to cover the verdict in a lawsuit brought against you, you may be able to buy "excess" liability insurance, to supplement your standard malpractice policy. This coverage is expensive, but sometimes worthwhile.

In addition to the costs of defending a lawsuit that is covered under the malpractice policy itself, the lawsuit may generate an investigation by your state licensing board. You can purchase supplemental coverage to pay for legal fees associated with any hearings before licensing boards. Further, you can be sued for your employee's mistake, under a "vicarious liability" or "agency" theory. Therefore, purchase a "vicarious liability" supplement, to give you coverage for the actions of all of your employees, including associate physicians, nurse practitioners and physician assistants.

Keep Copies of Policies

Retain copies of all insurance policies indefinitely, because claims can be brought against you years after the policy period expires.

Chapter 2: Avoiding Malpractice Lawsuits

Before the 1960s, doctors were held in high esteem, revered in a God-like manner. Patients never sued their physicians. That unique status no longer exists.

Doctors spend their time engulfed in lawsuits alleging a variety of "wrongs." Patients sue for negligence, lack of informed consent, wrongful death, wrongful life, wrongful pregnancy, slips and falls outside the office and violations of the Americans with Disabilities Act. Employees sue for sexual harassment, violations of the Age Discrimination in Employment Act, hostile work environment, discrimination, et cetera. The government sues physicians for alleged violations of OSHA, Stark Laws, HIPAA, in addition to fraud and abuse. The list goes on… and on… and on. This section is focused on helping you avoid being sued for malpractice.

When something goes wrong with a patient or loved one's care, it is human nature to want to hold someone accountable. Because physicians no longer have the intimate, personal relationship of yesteryear with their patients, often the treating physician is blamed for bad outcomes. Anger and unreasonable expectations drive malpractice suits as often as does poor quality of care. In fact, it is probably more often that the impersonal nature of the doctor's relationship with the patient, a feeling that the doctor is not on the patient's side, results in a lawsuit than actual bad medical care.

Statistics

For every 100 malpractice claims, only 55% result in a lawsuit. Of those 55%, more than half are dismissed by the court. Of those remaining in the system, only 5% end up being decided by a verdict, and the verdict is in favor of the doctor most of the time. So being sued does not automatically result in a verdict. However, you still need to take steps to avoid a malpractice lawsuit.

To Avoid Lawsuits

While it is not possible to avoid ever being sued, there are a number of steps that help. Communication, Respect and Good Charting are key. Patients who like you are less likely to sue.

Communication:

- See your hospital patients regularly.

- Return patient phone calls.

- Encourage questions during visits.

- Keep patients informed. Continue to communicate as the treatment continues.

- Be available to answer questions – during the day and evening as well. When this is not possible, ask a well-trained staff person to call the patient or patient's family as appropriate.

- Make sure that you and your patient are in agreement with what care should be given, how and when. Be on the same wavelength.

- Explain the diagnosis, tests and treatments slowly and carefully, allowing time for your explanations to sink in and be processed and understood. If necessary, ask if the patient wants you to talk to a family member.

- What you say and what the patient hears are often *far* apart. Talk in plain English that is geared to your patient's level of sophistication. Ask the patient to repeat what you have said.

- Put anything that could possibly be misunderstood into simple, preprinted materials. Figure out what the common questions are and make sure that you answer them, both orally and in writing.

- Be totally, gut-wrenchingly honest when answering patient questions. For example, saying that surgery is pain-free is not a good idea. Surgery *will* hurt.

- Ask patients for feedback about yourself, your office practices and your personnel. This gives them an opportunity to have input – positive criticism, if you will. Take their concerns seriously.

- If you are practicing in a small community, tell patients that there are limits to what you can do. Offer the option of going to a larger metropolitan center. Explain the potential benefits of the larger metropolis. Point out the additional time and expense of travel, and the obvious problem of being away from home.

- Be aware of institutional policies. In a recent case, a hospital had a very clear internal policy of terminating medicines after an initial prescribed course of pharmaceutical therapy, without a reevaluation by the doctor. The unaware doctor was held liable for the resulting injuries even though he had assumed the medications would continue to be given to the ill patient, since he was unaware of the hospital's policy of discontinuing medicine.

Respect:

- Treat patients in a caring and respectful manner.

- Do not be judgmental.

- Be sympathetic.

- Have a positive, honest, professional relationship with every patient.

- Be patient.

- Do not be distracted when you are with your patient despite the requirement to use computers and EMRs.

- Your bedside manner often makes the difference. Empathetic, easygoing doctors who establish a positive rapport with their patients and families are sued less often.

- Recognize that many patients and family members are scared – of the symptoms and of the potential prognosis. While you cannot alleviate all of their fears, you can sympathize with them. Be human.

- Have a patient-friendly office.

- Making appointments should be easy. Patients should be able to speak to a real person.

- Train your staff to smile, greet everyone calmly and look them in the eye, no matter how busy the office.

- Your office reception area is the first thing patients observe when they come for their first examination. In effect, your waiting room is a marketing tool, shaping the way patients see you and your practice. A professional looking reception area raises your patients' expectations, just as a bad waiting area makes a very negative impression. Make sure the office is clean and that there is comfortable seating.

- You want all patients, especially the ones who have difficulty ambulating or getting up from a sitting position, to be comfortable. The chairs should be in a contrasting color to the carpeting, especially if you have sight-impaired patients, because the contrast makes it easier for patients to see their seats. The last thing you need is to have a patient fall in your waiting room.

- Use the waiting area as a free marketing opportunity – offer educational materials.

- Understand that the patient has an expectation that he or she will be seen at the scheduled appointment time. After all, the patient's personal schedule is arranged around the appointment time given by the doctor's office.

- If you cannot avoid making the patient wait to see you, both the staff and physician should apologize. It is easy to picture a plaintiff's attorney using the long wait that the patient had as a reason that the doctor had to rush through the examination, thereby missing something that in turn resulted in the patient's injury.

- If your office always runs late, build in "extra' time to the schedule for patients who require more time than usual.

Good Charting:
- The health care provider knows a lawsuit is being considered when a request for a patient's chart is received. This does not necessarily mean that you are being sued – but certainly someone has gone to an attorney complaining about that patient's care.

- A good chart that shows the provider took the vital signs, asked questions and listened to the answers, ordered appropriate tests and medications and then followed up as necessary goes a long way to having the patient's attorney not file the contemplated lawsuit.

- Record all positive and negative findings on the chart. Record all prescription refills, telephone calls, and other interactions on the patient's chart. Put copies of e-mails and your responses to them in the chart as well. The more information you include, the better off you are in the long run.

- If you refer the patient to another doctor, document the referral, the reason for the referral and the plan of care after the referral. Record the fact that you told the patient why it was important to see the consultant, and that you told the patient the referral had to be done within a specific time frame. Your staff should send the clinical data to the referral doctor with the patient's consent.

- Document the fact that you gave informed consent for all events, major and minor alike, including "high risk" medications, minor surgical procedures et cetera. The mere fact that the chart reflects the informed consent is sometimes sufficient to overcome the issue of liability if you are sued. A recent Pennsylvania case held that a physician is not permitted to delegate the duty to obtain informed consent to a staff member or other professional.

- Improve your dictation skills. Your patient chart notes oftentimes become the tiebreaker in whether a plaintiff's attorney continues a lawsuit against you or not. Dictate in a quiet place, enunciate clearly, have your facts right, detail your interactions with the patient as well as your thoughts regarding the case. Remember that the chart you are dictating today may end up in front of a jury some day in the future. Always review what you have written. Errors are common when using dictation software with your EMR.

- Practice defensive medicine, which means changing the way you practice to decrease the likelihood of being sued.

- However, do not practice defensive medicine to the patient's detriment. Order only consults, tests and x-rays that are necessary. If there is a reasonable basis for ordering the tests, et cetera, however, you will be better protected by doing so.

Chapter 3: Types of Lawsuits: Medical Malpractice and Others

While most physicians fear medical malpractice lawsuits, there are endless ways that doctors can be sued. This chapter concentrates on malpractice actions, but includes other varieties of lawsuits at the end.

A doctor can be sued for malpractice under a variety of circumstances, all of which depend on state law. Most malpractice lawsuits are brought because the patient or the patient's family believes the physician has committed an error that has resulted in injury.

Should You Tell a Patient About Your Error?

We all know that sometimes the physician actually does make a mistake in patient care. There are several different schools of thought about whether a physician should tell a patient when the physician in fact has committed an error. The trend over recent years has been to disclose mistakes.

The AMA and some states now require disclosure of errors to patients. If you practice in such a state, the following discussion is rendered moot. If your state does not require disclosure, then although the doctor-patient relationship is a fiduciary one, based on trust, there are very different schools of thought on this subject of a physician's obligation to disclose:

- There is a school of thought that a physician who has actually caused the medical problem of which the patient is complaining should acknowledge that act, especially if there was a significant medical complication. Like all people, doctors sometimes make mistakes. Be sympathetic while you candidly acknowledge what happened, and explain what you can do to rectify the situation. You have an ethical duty to treat patients properly, with dignity and honesty, and failure to disclose a known error breaches the doctor's fiduciary duty to the patient.

Versus

- The second school of thought maintains that the patient is the person who is responsible to decide if there was a mistake.

Versus

- The third school, voiced by The Joint Commission, states that patients should be told about ordinary outcomes of care and unanticipated outcomes. The JC does not posit a concomitant responsibility to admit fault or liability.

Apology Laws

Apology laws are laws enacted by the states with the intention of mitigating the conflict a physician faces when trying to meet a patient's or family's desire for an apology while avoiding self-incrimination that can then be used in a medical malpractice suit against the physician. The intention of Apology Laws is to change traditional evidentiary rules by providing that the apology is not admissible in cases for medical malpractice. In other words, these laws encourage expressions of sympathy by a physician without the statement of condolence being misconstrued as an admission of liability.

It was initially assumed that allowing a physician to provide an apology for an error and/or bad medical outcome would decrease the number of lawsuits and the amount of awards. However, a recent Vanderbilt University (2017) study on this issue suggests that Apology Laws do not help physicians avoid malpractice payouts and do not reduce the number of claims that result in a lawsuit.

Approximately 36 states and the District of Columbia have Apology Laws. These laws differ among states and have their own nuances. You need to know what the law in your state allows you to say, and how to say it, to avoid having your gesture of concern and sympathy used against you in a medical malpractice lawsuit. Check with your healthcare attorney, state licensing board, or local medical society for the information.

Garden-Variety Medical Malpractice

Physicians may be sued for their negligence with regard to treatment of a patient, when that treatment of the patient is below the standard of care of doctors in the community. They may also be sued because of their roles as gatekeepers. These lawsuits are based on failure to diagnose, a delay in diagnosis, negligent referral to specialists or subspecialists, lack of referral to specialists or subspecialists, and premature discharge while patients are still ill. Beyond the "typical" malpractice lawsuits, there are many other legal theories that can be used by attorneys to sue doctors. We have broken these down into the more common ones being used presently.

Malpractice Lawsuits by Other Doctors

A defendant can "bring you in" via a "joinder complaint." For example, suppose your patient is seen by you, the primary care provider and by several specialists in consult. If that patient sues a single specialist but not you, the consultant's attorney can "join" you and/or the other specialists, alleging that your malpractice caused or contributed to cause the patient's problem.

Expert Witness

Depending on your state's law, expert witnesses generally can be sued under several theories:

- Rendering "friendly expert" testimony. Do not deviate from the accepted standards of medicine by falsely changing "real" medicine to fit the facts of the side that is paying you.
- For a mistake made in connection with the review and analysis of a claim.
- For perjury. Do not exaggerate your credentials.

Emotional Distress

Under many states' laws, physicians may be sued for severe emotional distress even if there is no physical negligence. A recent case held that a mother whose child was born with multiple abnormalities could sue the doctor who had failed to prepare her for the shock and distress of seeing the child.

Loss of Consortium

This claim relates to the deprivation of the benefits of a family relationship due to injuries caused by the healthcare provider. The deprivations recognized include the economic contributions of the injured spouse to the household, care and affection, and sexual relations. Since same-sex marriage became available in the United States, courts have extended loss of consortium claims to these unions.

Delegating Care to Others

You may be sued when you exercise control or supervision over others, such as hospital nurses who make a mistake, or for delegating responsibility to a non-doctor without providing adequate supervision. Further, you may be held responsible for a bad patient outcome where you have delegated your patient's care to another physician in a cross-coverage arrangement, if that doctor does not possess the appropriate competency to treat your patients with care.

You can be liable for the negligence of a doctor with whom you have entered into a joint venture, such as where both of you have combined your work efforts and/or your property in some fashion, and you each can exercise control over each other's actions.

Nonfeasance

Usually, you need a physician-patient relationship to be sued for malpractice. However, if you are on call and refuse to go to the hospital to treat a patient, are you liable if harm results? Liability may attach even if you have never provided care, treatment or advice, if a court finds that you have breached a duty of care.

Negligent Referrals

A serious problem arises if you refer patients to a doctor who causes them harm. The standard by which you, the referring doctor, are measured is a matter of state law. As a general rule, the measuring rod is whether a reasonable physician would have known that the consultant's performance record was poor. If a reasonable physician would have known this and you make the referral nonetheless, and injury results, you might be held responsible to pay compensatory damages. These damages are designed to "compensate" or make the injured person "whole" from the resulting injuries. Make sure you know how referring physicians perform professionally before you make a referral.

Depending on your state's law, it is also possible that you could be sued for punitive damages, to "punish" you for acting so irresponsibly in making a referral. Malpractice insurance policies rarely pay punitive damages so you would be personally responsible to pay any punitive damages awarded. The lesson to be learned here is to be extremely careful in making referrals to other doctors.

Yet all doctors have patients who need to be referred to other doctors to handle certain medical problems that are beyond the scope of the original physician's clinical expertise. In an effort to make prudent referrals, investigate any doctor you have never referred patients. Ask around. Seek recommendations from other physicians in your area. Ask the ED nurses. Investigate the doctor's complication rate versus the number of cases treated. If you have already made some referrals to a given doctor, seek patient feedback and ask about the care the referring doctor has given your patients before you continue with that referral pattern.

If you believe you will never be held responsible for making a negligent referral because you know how tough your hospital is credentialing process is, think again. Many of the social problems that tend to move doctors down that slippery slope from "normal" to "impaired" did not exist when the physician first applied for staff privileges. Although the initial process is often very stringent, once a doctor gets privileges, the doctor tends to remain on staff. Do not use the hospital credentialing process as a gauge for competency or other attributes.

Employee Actions

An employer-physician may be held liable for the negligent actions of an employee under a theory of "vicarious liability." That is, if a physician's staff member negligently carries out the doctor's orders or negligently cares for a patient, the physician may be sued. Private medical practices may be held liable for their partners' and associates' negligence.

Actions by Insurers

To avoid being sued for bad decisions by patient insurance companies, advocate vigorously for your patients, challenging authorization delays and denials for services you believe are reasonably necessary for the patient's care, and follow up with any administrative appeals on your patient's behalf. Write to the insurer's utilization review committee or medical director and outline any problems you perceive. Be prepared to show that during each step of the denial process, you advocated vigorously for the patient.

Document everything you do for your patient when you believe that the insurer is not upholding its part of the contract with your patient. Remind the patient that he or she does have the option to pay out of pocket for the treatment. Keep the patient informed about the status of the insurance issues.

In addition to the doctor, patients are able to sue their health insurer, alleging that the insurer "forced" their doctors to act a certain way. If the doctor was an actual employee or even an "apparent agent" of the insurer, the insurer can be held vicariously liable for the doctor's actions.

Bad Office Management

Doctors and potentially their employees can be held liable for problems caused by incompetent office staff. If the employer cannot get the employee to act properly, or vice versa, find a different employee or employer.

Lack of Adequate Assistants

Never use someone who is not properly credentialed as an assistant for a procedure or surgery you are performing. You have a duty to have adequately trained and, where indicated, appropriately credentialed, staff at all times.

Social Media

Healthcare providers need to be careful in their use of social media. There are several federal laws that protect patients in the health care arena from improper use of information on social media. The most common problem is a HIPAA breach. This occurs when the acquisition, access, use, or disclosure of Patient Health Information (PHI) is not authorized.

Public posting of names, addresses, pictures, et cetera of patients is obviously prohibited. In addition, so is posting of birth and death dates, Social Security numbers, telephone numbers, email addresses and any other information that would be sufficient to allow someone to identify the patient from that data.

You can be fired, your employer can be sued, you can be reprimanded by your medical board, et cetera for your inappropriate use of social media in general. What is said or published can be used against you in a medical malpractice case. The list goes on. You need to maintain patient privacy and confidentiality at all times. Always act professionally and stay within these boundaries.

Whatever interactions you have with patients directly must be professional. If you see unprofessional content online posted by others, you must bring that to the attention of the poster or even report the posting to the appropriate authority. Remember that your online content remains there for all to access.

Elder Abuse

An increasing number of lawsuits are being brought against doctors and hospitals alike for elder abuse and ignoring patient wishes, especially those who wish "to die with dignity." The picture of a chronically ill patient who clearly and unequivocally told everyone, including the doctor, of his desire to die at home surrounded by loved ones is juxtaposed with the patient full of intravenous medications and tubes, suffering, on drugs, finally dying in the sterile-smelling cold hospital room. This can result in a large verdict, especially when the family explains how they went broke struggling to pay for the costs of the unwanted treatment.

Some of these cases are brought under the theory of "battery," which is generally defined as the unwanted touching by virtue of rending the unwanted treatment. Others cases are brought alleging "wrongful living" and still others allege the doctor's intentional or negligent interference with the patient's legal right to die.

It is amazing when you think about it – you can be sued for allowing a patient to die, via a lawsuit for wrongful death, as well as for saving the patient's life, via a case for wrongful life. Sometimes you have to feel that the cards are stacked against you. So what is the solution? Communicate with your patients, document their wishes and discussions and then follow through to the best of your ability.

PDR Warnings and Medication Inserts

The entries in the Physician's Desk Reference and inserts into drug packaging are designed to comply with the Food and Drug Administration rules and to limit the manufacturer's liability. In and of itself, the failure to adhere to the PDR warnings does not mean that a physician has breached the standard of care. However, the entries and inserts do show what a doctor knew or should have known about a particular drug.

Keep abreast of the FDA prescription drug warnings and recalls. When there is a newly approved therapy in your field, read the label to ensure that you fully understand the potential problems associated with its use. Doctors need to be familiar with any significant studies on the side effects or interactions of the prescribed drug with other medications. Always weigh the benefits and risks of giving a patient a certain medication. Remember to personally give informed consent so the patient understands fully and completely all potential significant adverse side effects associated with a medication.

Medication Errors

Many lawsuits involve medication errors. Interactions between medications must be anticipated, monitored and when necessary, appropriately corrected. Since drug interactions may also occur between your prescribed medications and herbal and other over-the-counter medications, you are required to ask the appropriate questions to determine what "medications" your patient is taking, right down to vitamins.

Make sure you explain the difference between brand-name and generic medications. Tell your patients to read the drug labels and document the discussion. If you are prescribing "off-label" use, you may need to obtain written informed consent. Tell your patients of the potential drug-food and drug-drug interactions and document the discussion.

Depending on the age of your patients, consider asking all patients to bring in all of the medications, vitamins and any "extra" daily medicines, so that they can be reviewed and discussed during each appointment. Carefully monitor your patients for known side effects and educate your patients about their medicines, including potential side effects and adverse drug interactions. Consider distributing written materials that the patients can take home with them and document the fact that you have given the materials.

Pain Management

There have also been a number of lawsuits involving pain management – or more specifically, for causing needless suffering by failing to prescribe sufficient medication. You must carefully listen to your patient's needs and if you cannot manage the pain, refer the patient to someone else who can provide the appropriate care.

This has become a complex issue, especially given the current opioid crisis across the United States. A jury awarded $17.6 million in compensatory and punitive damages to a couple who had filed a medical malpractice lawsuit against a physician for overprescribing opioid pain medication.

Pharmaceutical Combinations

You may find, as many doctors in the past few years have discovered, that a particular drug combination you have prescribed in the past is causing major physical problems to the general public. If this is the case, notify those patients to whom you have prescribed the drug of the need for examination. Post notice of the problem in your waiting area. Write to patients to whom you gave the medication and explain the problem.

Describe how evidence of a problem has been noted in some patients. Give whatever information is necessary so that a reasonable patient reading your letter would understand the need for an evaluation. "It is important to me that you remain healthy. Please contact a physician for a follow-up appointment. This should be done immediately. You should have a full medical evaluation." Mail the letter certified mail, return receipt requested, and keep a copy of the letter in the patient chart.

Preventative Medications

Be careful to document recommendations that you make regarding preventative medicine, including what educational materials you have distributed.

Allergic Reactions

It is not enough to just ask and answer routine questions when it comes to allergies. There was a case involving a peanut allergy that resulted in a $10 million verdict. The parents acknowledged they knew it was dangerous for their son to eat peanuts and so they had tried to prevent the child's exposure to peanuts. The problem was that the doctors had not fully warned them of the danger of anaphylactic shock.

Physicians are obligated to develop a thorough plan to avoid future allergic reactions. Tell the patient and family members what to do if a reaction occurs. Remind parents to tell all those charged with their child's care, including relatives, babysitters and school officials, of the potential ramifications of the allergy. Document your chart thoroughly.

Driving and Medications

Health care providers are responsible to warn patients when performing tests, administering vaccinations, et cetera if you believe the person may faint or be dangerous to others. Physicians are responsible to warn patients that they should not drive while taking certain medications because the drugs could affect their ability to drive well and they could injure third parties. When you see any risk to a third party, tell the patient not to drive and make the patient bring an adult to drive home.

A doctor owes a limited duty to third parties (such as pedestrians and other drivers) who are foreseeably at risk from a patient's decision to drive. That physician must warn the patient of the known side effects of medications the physician has prescribed that might impair the patient's ability as a motorist. If you permit a patient to drive under inappropriate circumstances, you can be held liable to the patient and/or any third parties who are injured if your patient causes an accident. As always, document the chart.

Driver Safety

Physicians are responsible to ensure the safety of those who may be affected by patients. In most states, this responsibility extends to notifying drivers' licensing bureaus of the identity of patients who are no longer capable of safe driving. For example, Pennsylvania created a Medical Advisory Board to define disorders that may affect the ability of a person to drive safely. You need to verify that your state permits you to provide this information to the Department of Transportation without the patient's permission, so that you are immune from civil and criminal liability.

If there is any question that your patient has a mental or physical disability or disorder that may render the patient incapable of safe highway driving, consult with your local state medical society or your health care attorney about how to proceed.

Other Danger to Third Parties

If your patient has threatened a third party, you may have to warn that third party even if your warning breaches patient confidentiality. Similarly, if your patient has a contagious disease, you may be obligated to notify other parties at potential risk for injury. Because the laws on such matters differ radically from state to state, consult your local medical society or health care attorney if such issues arise in your practice.

Clearing Patients for Surgeries

Be careful when you fill out pre-op forms for people who are undergoing surgical procedures. If the patient is injured because of surgery that should not have been done to someone in your patient's medical condition, you can be sued, based on your negligence in completing the paperwork.

Sports and Health Clubs

Clearing a patient for strenuous workouts in health clubs and on athletic fields can result in a lawsuit, on the basis of your failure to have foreseen that an existing medical problem made the person an inappropriate sports competitor. Only sign forms for actual patients whose medical history you know after a full examination and evaluation.

Informed Consent

Informed consent is a legal concept built on the established principle that every adult of sound mind has a right to determine what is to be done with his or her own body. Patients are allowed to refuse to agree to what the medical practitioner is planning to do to the patient. It is more than getting a patient to sign a form – there needs to be actual communication between the patient and the doctor.

Going back to the early 1970s, courts in some states declared that a physician who performs an operation without advising the patient of all of the material risks, benefits and alternatives to certain medical procedures can be liable for having committed a battery. That is, by not giving informed consent, the physician is deemed to have engaged in the unlawful touching of the patient, without consent. In other states, not giving informed consent is deemed to be negligence.

Regardless of the theory used by your state, if you fail to give informed consent when appropriate, the patient may be entitled to damages, even where the procedure itself was done appropriately. That is, informed consent is an entirely distinct issue from medical malpractice.

Informed Consent Versus Medical Malpractice

Failure to adequately inform a patient of all material risks, benefits and alternatives to a surgical procedure subjects a health care practitioner to a claim for damage if an adverse result occurs, even if the doctor performed appropriately and within the standard of care for that community. The standard for failure to give informed consent is usually entirely different from that of malpractice, which is a legal concept based on providing medical care at a level below that of other doctors in the general community that results in injury to the plaintiff/patient.

Informed Refusal

The flip side of informed consent is "informed refusal." If your patient refuses to consent to treatments you recommend, this presents the opposite problem. Make sure your patient signs a form documenting the patient's refusal to consent to the treatment, and then note in the chart both the refusal and attendant circumstances.

Discrimination

Title VII of the Civil Rights Act of 1964 prohibits doctors from singling out patients based on race, gender (sex), religion or national origin. Doctors are not permitted to engage in practices that may have a discriminatory effect or impact on patients because of their race or national origin. There are usually state laws as well that prohibit discrimination.

This is a powerful deterrent to those who might consider discriminating against non-English speaking patients. Doctors must deal with the "natural" language barriers to care that potentially discriminate against non-English speaking patients and which deprive these patients of medical services that are as effective as those given to the rest of the community.

If you get federal funding (e.g., if you participate in Medicare or Medicaid), you must provide interpreters for patients who have "limited English proficiency." This includes hiring interpreters for language and also for deaf patients. Note the interpreter's name, address, and telephone number, and interpreter identification number, if they have one, in the patient's chart.

Performing medical procedures on patients with whom you cannot effectively communicate is dangerous. Harm caused by not overcoming language barriers can rise to a claim of medical negligence as well as a charge of lack of informed consent. Performing a medical procedure on a person who has not given effective informed consent can result in the doctor being liable for the tort of "battery," usually defined as an unlawful touching.

Abandonment

The law forbids you from abandoning your patients. The issues of when refusal to treat and dismissal of patients are viewed as patient abandonment become complicated in medical practices.

Sometimes the trouble of taking care of an individual patient who is paying for the care and treatment you render starts to outweigh the personal and financial benefits of being involved in that patient's care. Patients who are abusive, unruly and who do not heed your medical advice can become a liability to you. However, you must take certain steps to terminate the doctor-patient relationship properly by giving the appropriate notice in advance to the patient so you will not be liable for abandonment.

Discuss the problem first with the patient. Explain that your practice cannot tolerate continued missed appointments, inappropriate demands, cursing, loud behavior, adverse interactions with you and/or your staff or whatever the particulars are. Document the chart. If the problem behavior continues after a frank discussion, though, dismissal may be appropriate.

To avoid a lawsuit premised on abandonment, develop a form letter to send patients, including the following:

- That you can no longer provide medical care because of the differences in philosophy. Do not cite all of the gory details. Be succinct and clear. For example, if the patient is rude, you may say that the patient's behavior has been disruptive to your practice, upsetting your patients and staff alike.
- That the patient should find a new physician to deal with the particular type of medical care that the patient will need in the future.
- That the patient can contact the local medical society (and include the telephone number and address) so the patient can obtain other doctors in your area of practice and locale.
- That the patient can seek assistance at the local hospital, (include the telephone number and address).
- That you will make the patient's medical records available to a new physician upon receipt of a signed release of records form, and explain the

method you have set up to transfer the records. Many doctors include a blank release.

- That you will remain available for a certain number of days (usually thirty (30) from the date of mailing of the letter in the event an emergency medical problem arises. Your local medical society can tell you the minimum number of days of advance notice that you must give your patient so you can avoid being legally liable for abandoning the patient.

- That if the patient contacts you within this time period seeking emergency assistance or interim care, you will provide that care as you are required to by law.

Note that sometimes there are special circumstances that require more care. For example, treatment of a patient who has an acute condition or is in a critical or life-threatening condition must continue until the treatment is no longer necessary or the patient gets a new doctor and the records are released to the doctor, whichever occurs first. Similarly, you cannot terminate a pregnant woman too close to her due date unless she gets a new physician first.

Mail the letter dismissing the patient from your practice, certified mail, return receipt requested, so that the patient will be required to sign for the delivery.

Include a copy of the discharge letter and the signed receipt showing delivery in the patient's chart. Also keep a memorandum of your rendition of what transpired giving rise to the dismissal. If your staff observed the interactions, include the staff members' separately written statements in their own words detailing the matter. Your chart should be very clear about the entire situation.

Good Samaritans

Although presumably most of the time you see patients and render medical assistance within the confines of your office or hospital setting, there will inevitably be times throughout your career that you are faced with a stranger who needs emergency medical help with whom you have no traditional doctor-patient relationship. Generally, there is no legal duty to help a stranger in need. While physicians may choose to help those in acute distress, they are usually not required to do so. Again, because each state is different, seek local counsel.

The law is fairly clear that you will be protected if you volunteer your services in the full meaning of the word "volunteer." The problem is that doctors do not carry portable offices along with their good judgment. Their medical equipment and other useful items are missing when the sudden out-of-office emergency arises. All doctors have at those times is their medical knowledge, along with their good ethics and moral judgment that it is wrong to let a human suffer when they might be able to help.

"Good Samaritan" laws are statutes that exempt from legal liability a person (like the physician) who voluntarily renders aid to another who is in imminent danger but who negligently causes injury while rendering the aid. Although "Good Samaritan" laws differ from state to state to some extent, these laws provide the standard, by which you will be judged if you render emergency services to a non-patient.

Normally as long as you voluntarily provide services outside your ordinary medical practice in an emergency where you have no preexisting duty to provide that assistance, you are insulated or protected from liability for ordinary negligence. Most states apply this protection only in those instances where you have not asked to be paid, do not expect to be paid and in fact, have not been paid. Therefore, if you do help a person in an emergency on the street, in a restaurant, or in a friend's house and you are paid for the treatment rendered, you generally can be held responsible for your negligence.

Gross Negligence Exception

Where a doctor is grossly negligent, acting in total disregard of the risks attendant to the situation, most state laws allow the patient to sue for the injuries sustained. Gross negligence is usually defined as willful, wanton or reckless misconduct. It is far more than a mere mistake or inadvertence. It is highly unreasonable conduct. Gross negligence is evidenced usually by the patient being left in a substantially worse medical condition after the treatment than before.

Giving Aid During Airplane Flights

An interesting problem occurs when you are asked to render medical assistance during an airline flight. The general goal with in-flight medical help is to stabilize the passenger until the flight ends. In 1998, the Aviation Medical Assistance Act was enacted, providing "Good Samaritan" protection to medically trained passengers who help other passengers during the course of a flight. This statute requires that the medically trained passenger not submit a bill in order to be covered by the Act. Do keep a record of what you did and document it in a medical record when you return home.

False Claims

All medical practitioners, whether in private practice or in academia, need to understand the basic concepts of the federal False Claims Act. Being paid with funds from the United States Treasury (e.g., for services rendered to Medicare or Medicaid patients) for services or supplies that were not provided the way the claim states, or for which the provider is otherwise not entitled to payment, is a "false claim." The Office of the Inspector General ("OIG") uses a liberal interpretation in deciding what constitutes a "false claim."

False claims arise in these basic fact patterns:

- Knowingly submitting a false or fraudulent claim to the United States for payment;
- Knowingly using a false record or statement to get paid on a false or fraudulent claim; and
- Being part of a conspiracy (two (2) or more people working together) to defraud the United States by knowingly having a false or fraudulent claim allowed or paid.

"Knowingly" is defined as having actual knowledge that the information on the claim is false OR acting in reckless disregard of the truth or falsity of the information on the claim. That is, a careless provider who does not try to figure out the truth of the claim can be responsible for submitting a false claim because ignoring the obvious is not a defense.

Included as potential false claims are claims filed for items or services furnished by an individual or entity that the provider knew or should have known was on the "excluded list." All providers are required to check the exclusion status of individuals and entities the practice hires or contracts with, in advance of the hiring or contracting. If a practice hires someone and submits claims for payment of services rendered by the excluded person or entity, the practice could be subjected to penalties and potentially exclusion from the federal health care programs.

Therefore, it is incumbent upon the practice to check the List of Excluded Individuals and Entities on the OIG's Website, https://oig.hhs.gov/exclusions, and then document the efforts. Periodic reviews of all employees, vendors and contracts should be undertaken as well. Save copies of the search results in a separate file.

Violating the False Claims Act leads to civil penalties equal to 3 times the improper amount received, in addition to the refund of the improper amount, plus hefty fines per false claim. If the case is particularly egregious, the doctor can also be prohibited from participating in the Medicare program.

Antitrust and Stark Laws

Physicians' financial interests should never take precedence over patient care. Commercial ventures owned by doctors, including laboratories, radiology facilities and medical supply companies, have historically created the potential for economic abuse because they create conflicts of interest with patient care.

"Kickbacks," payments for referrals made to a medical practice, are illegal. The federal "anti-kickback" statute prohibits doctors from knowingly and willfully:

- Soliciting, receiving, offering or paying any kind of remuneration
- In return for referring someone for services, recommending or arranging the purchase, lease or even ordering of any item
- Where the service or item may be paid, in whole or part, by a federal health care program.

This statute takes on special meaning if you are thinking of supplementing your income with an additional business arrangement. If even a single purpose of a relationship between a hospital or any other health care facility or service and a doctor is to induce referrals, both parties are violating the federal anti-kickback statute.

Also, avoid entering into "outside" business relationships with referral sources and/or their spouses. The business relationship may also raise red flags with the Office of Inspector General if you have a referral relationship. Everything must be at arms-length and at fair market value. You need to be free to refer patients to the doctor of your choice.

The federal government passed Stark I and II (referred to collectively as "the Stark laws") to deal specifically with physician self-referral. These laws prohibit physicians from:

- Referring Medicare or Medicaid patients **To** an entity for the provision of "designated health services" (including "clinical laboratory services"; "physical therapy services"; "occupational therapy services"; "radiology services, including magnetic resonance imaging, computerized axial tomography scans, and ultrasound services"; "radiation therapy services and supplies"; "durable medical equipment and supplies"; "parenteral and enteral nutrients, equipment, and supplies"; "prosthetics, orthotics, and prosthetic devices and supplies"; "home health services"; "outpatient prescription drugs"; "inpatient and outpatient hospital services"; and "outpatient speech-language pathology services.)

- If the physician (or a member of the doctor's immediate family) has a financial relationship (direct or indirect) with that entity
- Unless the doctor can prove that an exception ("safe harbor") has been met.

Whereas traditional fraud and abuse statutes require the government to prove illegal intent to refer or to receive payments for referrals, the latest Stark laws make intent irrelevant in determining whether an impermissible referral has been made.

Violations of the statute can result in criminal fines, incarceration and/or the imposition of stiff civil penalties. In addition, a physician violating the law can be excluded from participating in federal health care programs in the future. Be careful!

Antitrust Laws

The Sherman Antitrust Act of 1890 gives the federal

government the right to bring civil actions against individual health care providers to stop violations of this federal law.

Some common violations include:

- Forming combinations, contracts and conspiracies that restrain trade
- Price-fixing
- Tying products and/or services to each other
- Exclusive dealing
- Boycotts (concerted refusals to deal)
- Mergers that limit competition
- Monopolization
- Dividing up a market (market allocation)

Antitrust law is extremely complex, especially as it involves the healthcare industry. The good news for doctors is that state legislatures can pass laws exempting doctors from the antitrust laws, and some have been taking this step.

Lawsuits Involving Your Property

You may be sued by someone who is injured as a result of being on your property, which really has nothing to do with your being a doctor. You must purchase liability insurance to cover injuries that occur outside and inside your medical office. If you own the property, the lease you enter with your tenant usually determines who is responsible to pay for injuries sustained on the property. If you lease the property, again, the lease also usually governs.

However, you should review your local and state laws as well. For example, many cities require commercial tenants to keep sidewalks free of hazards. This includes ice and snow. In some cities, a commercial tenant will be responsible, even if the lease itself shifts the burden to the landlord. That is, it is possible for both the landlord and tenant to be "jointly and severally liable" to an innocent third party.

Practicing Beyond Your Expertise

You are not permitted to practice outside your area of expertise. More and more primary care doctors are being asked to do things beyond the scope of their training. If you practice beyond the scope of your prior medical training, you will be held to the standard of the specialist who would provide the same service that you are providing. That is, if a primary care physician or other provider interprets an x-ray, the standard against which the provider is judged is that of a radiologist, not a primary provider.

Before you provide services just because an insurance company or a patient tells you to do them, think again. Check your insurance policy and reexamine your liability. If a reasonably qualified doctor or specialist would have made the diagnosis sooner, you will be liable for ensuing injuries.

Chapter 4: Defending Lawsuits

Being sued is one of the most gut-wrenching experiences a medical professional can experience. However, most of the time, the plaintiff's attorney either drops the case, the court dismisses the case or the doctor wins the case. Most cases never go to trial and those that do are won by the doctor the majority of the time. The odds are greater that the lawsuit will be unsuccessful.

Preliminary Steps Before a Lawsuit is Initiated

If a plaintiff's attorney contacts you to casually discuss a case, beware. The attorney is not your friend. The more you talk and the more information you give, the greater the chance of your being sued. Anything you say can be used against you later and taken out of context.

Not all subpoenas are equally binding. A court order signed by a judge is usually binding, but one signed by a lawyer may not be. HIPAA governs the release of patient records, but is generally not applicable to records sought in response to a state medical board. The filing of a lawsuit by a patient usually waives HIPAA as well. However, consult with your attorney before releasing any medical records.

Sometimes you are subpoenaed to appear in a trial against someone else because of your capacity as a hospital employee or as some other "nonparty" witness. Be very careful giving testimony, because the attorney can potentially add you as a defendant to the lawsuit at a later point in time. Contact your medical malpractice insurance carrier immediately for advice as to the best way to handle the subpoena.

If a lawyer writes to you and asks for a chart, you must receive a patient's signed release as well. Although most states allow you to release a patient chart upon presentment of the signed release alone, check with your local medical society to see if a subpoena is required in your state. Again, you need a signed, current HIPAA release.

Your chart can be your best friend. A well-documented patient chart that shows you have done everything a reasonable physician could or would do makes many a lawsuit disappear. If not, your case will progress to a discovery stage, where each side will attempt to find out everything possible about the other side's position, and then eventually to trial unless it is dismissed or otherwise resolved.   However, assume for the moment that you actually get sued. What happens?

The Lawsuit Starts: Service of the Complaint

You will find out about the lawsuit when you are "served." "Service of process" is the legal term used for receiving the initial pleadings from the attorney for the plaintiff, the person who has started the lawsuit. Sometimes service is accomplished by the Sheriff knocking on your door. Other times, the paperwork arrives in the mail. The manner in which you are served with the initial documents from the plaintiff is mandated by the rules of the court in your jurisdiction (your geographic area).

Avoiding service will not help – eventually you will be served. Trying to avoid service is ridiculous. It is less embarrassing to be served the first time around than to have a process server show up in your busy waiting room in the middle of patient hours.

Usually the first paper you are served with is a "Complaint," a written summary of reasons the plaintiff is suing you. Sometimes instead, you are served with a "Writ of Summons," explaining that a lawsuit may be filed against you at a later point in time. Writs are usually filed when the time period within which the lawsuit can be commenced (the "statute of limitations" period) has almost expired. The plaintiff's attorney will still have to file a Complaint, but this Writ "satisfies" the statute of limitations.

The first thing you should do when you are served is to remain calm. Panicking will not help. We repeat... do NOT panic. Being sued is not a crisis. That is why you have been paying those hefty malpractice insurance coverage premiums. Unfortunately, being sued is part of doing business as a doctor in the United States these days.

Call Your Malpractice Carrier

Call your malpractice carrier immediately. Because your professional liability insurance contract probably obligates you to do this, failure to contact the insurance company may relieve the carrier of responsibility to defend the lawsuit and pay any verdict. Also, there is always a specific time within which you must file an "Answer" or some other court paperwork, so prompt forwarding of the legal papers to your insurance carrier is imperative. There is no reason to lose your case from the start.

Contact Your Attorney

Your carrier will retain an attorney to represent your interests. Communicate with this attorney as soon as you get the name. The lawyer may ask you to fax or e-mail a copy of the paperwork you have received so far, and then arrange a meeting to review the facts, obtain copies of your records, explain the legal procedures and process, et cetera. Try to get the attorney to come to your office for all meetings, at your convenience. The attorney is usually happy to do this because the malpractice carrier is paying the attorney hourly for the work, and the attorney can bill for all travel time. However, you must alter your schedule to make yourself available for all meetings with your attorney. Cooperation and communication with your attorney is crucial for your defense.

Complaint, Answer and Other Preliminaries

Review the Complaint carefully to determine what the plaintiff is alleging you did. Your attorney will decide whether to file "Preliminary Objections" to the Complaint, complaining of technical problems with the drafting, or to just file an Answer.

Interacting with Your Attorney

Read carefully anything that the attorney gives you to sign, even though your attorney has prepared it. It is your lawsuit, and you need to remain involved in the case. Ask the attorney any questions that you have after you review the documents the lawyer has prepared.

Be open and honest with your attorney. Be on top of the case and cooperate. Tell your attorney you want copies of everything that is received. Read whatever you get from the attorney. Educate your attorney – explain the facts and your theory of what happened. Ask your attorney for his/her theory of the case. Listen carefully and explain any holes you see in the logic.

Be available to your attorney. Help the attorney prepare your defense by giving the attorney all of the information possible about the medical issues that are involved in the case. Review the medical records carefully and then explain what care you gave and chose not to give the patient. The attorney needs to understand what you did and why you did it in order to respond to the Complaint properly. While the attorney understands the law, you understand medicine. Unless you are both a doctor and a lawyer, you probably will not have command of both disciplines, and neither will your attorney.

Patient Confidentiality

The lawsuit acts as a waiver of the duty of confidentiality you owe the plaintiff to some extent, at least as far as the specific medical condition or problems that gave rise to the lawsuit are concerned. Physicians are allowed to discuss the matter with their defense attorneys and are allowed to give the attorney the patient's chart and any accompanying documentation that may be relevant to the defense of the case. Interestingly enough, you are probably also allowed to discuss the case with your own psychiatrist, psychologist or medical doctor, because those conversations would be protected under your own doctor-patient privilege.

Because the lawsuit is a matter of public record, anyone who wants to learn about the details can read the pleadings filed of record. However, anything that is not part of the "four corners" of the documents the plaintiff filed is still protected by the doctor-patient confidentiality duty. While it is "normal" to tell your office staff that you have been sued, by whom and for what, remind them that you cannot talk about it and neither should they.

Although it is "legal" to discuss the case with friends, family, and co-workers, as long as you do not disclose the patient's name and any specifics of the lawsuit, limit your discussions to your lawyer. The more you talk, the more problems you may cause. You should avoid talking about the patient's condition to others, including "co-defendants" (other doctors or hospitals who were sued along with you).

Problems with Your Attorney

Although the insurance company is paying the attorney, you are the client and you have a right to be properly represented. If you are not satisfied with the attorney, talk to the insurance carrier. The company may give you a different attorney if your concerns are legitimate (lack of experience, major personality conflict, et cetera.).

Do Not Hide or Transfer Assets

Usually creditors cannot get assets held in joint names with your spouse. However, do not rush out and transfer everything to your spouse's name as soon as you are sued. Many states consider a transfer of an asset after a lawsuit is initiated to be a "fraudulent" transfer, which results in a string of legal problems.

Multiple Defendants

Many malpractice lawsuits are brought against more than one defendant at a time. If the different defendants have the same insurance carrier, a common defense can be quite beneficial – all of you are on the same team. However, it may not work out that way.

Each doctor who is sued has a personal stake in the outcome, and so each doctor wants what is best for that doctor. Often the different defendants want to engage in name calling and blaming. They end up being their own worst enemies. Your attorney will monitor the status of your co-defendant's case so ask to be kept informed.

Hiring a Separate Attorney

Many physicians also choose to retain their own attorney, in addition to the insurance company's defense attorney. Hiring your own private defense attorney is an expensive proposition, because you will have to pay your private attorney hourly. There are many good reasons to spend this money:

- If several of you are being sued together and the same insurer is mounting a "joint defense." By hiring an attorney of your own, you will protect your own interests from being trampled in the process.

- If the Complaint alleges that you did something intentionally to the plaintiff.
- If the lawsuit involves just peer review or licensing problems, unless you have paid extra to have this rider added to your malpractice policy. If there is any chance the issues underlying the administrative peer review or licensing action might form the basis for a malpractice suit, the carrier might pay for a defense lawyer for you even if you did not purchase the rider.
- If there is a chance that the jury verdict may exceed the limits of your coverage (an "excess verdict"). Your insurance company attorney will tell you if an excess verdict is a potential. Excess verdicts are rare, probably because attorneys discover the policy limits during the course of the lawsuit and every effort is made to settle the matter within those limits. This does not mean that the lawsuit has to settle within policy limits though. If it does not, you have to pay the difference above your malpractice policy limits directly to the plaintiff. Some states allow your wages to be garnished to pay off the balance, and some allow the seizure of certain retirement funds. Most states will not force

the sale of property owned by you and your spouse as "tenants by the entireties" to pay the balance of the judgment.

Discovery Stage

This stage allows each side to learn about the other's case. There can be written questions (Interrogatories), oral questions (Depositions) and Requests for Production of Documents (asking for specific pieces of paper, like the office chart, your CV, et cetera) seeking to discover the facts of the case.

Most commonly, depositions are used in medical malpractice cases to gather and share information between the parties. This is a very important part of the case itself. A good deposition can actually stop a case dead in its tracks. Do not take this stage lightly. A deposition is the other side's opportunity to get answers to a series of questions, under oath.

Prepare carefully for the deposition. Review all of the documents that you have received and that your attorney has filed. Meet with your attorney at least once, to review the clinical records, the documents, the kinds of questions that will likely be asked, et cetera. Be prepared to discuss your educational background, employment history, your practice training and your professional experience.

Most depositions occur in an attorney's office and seem casual. Do not be lulled into a false sense of friendliness. The plaintiff's attorney is only going to get paid if the plaintiff wins. It is in the plaintiff's attorney's best interest to make you comfortable enough to trick you into blurting out something that you should not say.

By the time your deposition occurs, you will already know the plaintiff's version of the facts. Although depositions are not held in courtrooms, a court stenographer will transcribe all of the questions and the answers as well. You will end up with a typed transcript of the questioning. When the actual courtroom trial starts, your answers can come back to haunt you if you answer differently at trial than you did during the deposition. Therefore, the need to prepare for your deposition should be quite clear.

A major problem with depositions is that doctors want to defend themselves at the deposition, and tell their story. This is not what happens at a deposition. You will be asked a series of questions, sometimes in no seeming order, and all you should do is answer the question that is asked. Do not elaborate. Just answer. Doctors want to volunteer information. Resist this at all costs. Let the attorney ask the question and you answer it and nothing more. The questions will not be telling a full story about the experience – sometimes a plaintiff's attorney just concentrates on a single part of the events.

If you do not have a recollection of a particular event, do not guess. Listen to the question carefully because you need to make sure that you are answering that question. The deposition transcript will not reflect the fact that you took an extra moment to answer the questions. So be thoughtful, slow and clear. Keep a respectful tone to your voice, and use good body language. Resisting glaring and snarling.

Plaintiff attorneys love arrogant, obnoxious doctors – and the first chance they get to find out the doctor's personality is at the deposition. Be down-to-earth. This gives the plaintiff's attorney reason to think about whether it is really worth it to continue the case. Look the lawyer in the eye while answering so you project your honesty and confidence.

A court reporter usually transcribes the entire deposition, so that the contents will be available at a later date to be read out loud. Whatever you say can and will be used against you. After the deposition is completed, you will be given a written copy of the deposition to review for inaccuracies in the transcription of the words said during the deposition. Read this carefully and note any problems.

If several of you are sued, think! If you can attend your co-defendant's deposition first, you will see how the plaintiff's counsel works, and you will be better prepared for your own turn. Ask your attorney to review copies of your co-defendant's deposition transcript in advance of your own deposition. Another great benefit of actually attending your co-defendant's deposition is that your co-defendant is less likely to point the finger at you if you are physically in the room while the co-defendant is being deposed.

Experts

Often your attorney will hire various experts to help defend you. There are several different types of experts routinely used in cases for different purposes:

- To state whether or not you breached the standard of medical care in your community. This expert usually has to be a physician who practices in your own specialty.
- Experts for causation, to help your attorney determine whether there is a cause and effect

relationship between the care you gave and the injuries and damages sustained.

- To deal with general damage issues, such as life expectancy and the cost of future medical care.

Pre-trial Motions

There are often motions that both attorneys file in advance of trial, and before the trial starts, the judge will render a decision. Depending on the results, certain testimony will or will not be allowed to be heard during the trial itself.

For example, if you are sued and you do not have Board Certification, the negative image that will be created could work against you. Before plaintiff's counsel brings up the fact that you have not passed the Board Certification, your lawyer will file a "pretrial motion" with the court. This will ask the court to prevent the plaintiff from asking any questions about Board Certification, based on the irrelevance of the exam results.

The judge will determine whether the being Board certified would help the jury determine the relevant issues in the case itself, or whether the fact that you do not have Board certification would be prejudicial to you by making the jury believe that your failure is more significant than it really is.

Many courts hold that whether you had passed or failed the examinations has no bearing on whether you departed from the appropriate standard of care in a particular case.

The Actual Trial

Before a trial actually starts, you will have plenty of opportunity to discuss strategy with your lawyer, who will also explain the stages of the trial. Generally, trials happen in this order:

- Voir dire, when the judge or attorneys ask prospective jurors a number of questions to determine their fitness to serve as jury members.
- Plaintiff's opening statement, where plaintiff's attorney tells the jury (or the judge alone if there is no jury) what the plaintiff intends to prove during the course of the trial.
- Defendant's opening statement, where defense counsel explains the defense version of the events.
- Plaintiff's "case in chief," which starts with the direct examination of witnesses that the plaintiff's counsel calls to the stand to support plaintiff's version of the facts. Some of the witnesses will include the plaintiff, family members and even friends who are able to testify about the patient's

condition and suffering. Your attorney will be permitted to "cross examine" those witnesses.

- Plaintiff will inevitably present at least one expert who will inform the jury that you acted improperly in caring for the patient and that your actions were "below the standard of care of a reasonable physician in your community" and that your breach was a substantial factor in causing the harm.

- Your attorney will cross-examine the expert, asking how often he or she testifies, how much of his or her salary comes from expert work, whether he or she is a plaintiff's expert only, et cetera. The thrust of this line of questions is to demonstrate the expert is a hired gun, shading testimony when necessary to keep the money rolling in.

- After the plaintiff has presented all of the witnesses for his or her side, then your side starts.

- Defense counsel will call witnesses as well, and conduct direct examination. Plaintiff's attorney will be permitted to cross-examine them.

- You will probably be called as a witness for your side. Be genuine, down-to-earth, compassionate and human. Let the jury get to know you as a doctor and a person. Relate to your attorney and make the jury understand you were doing your best at all times for the plaintiff and all of your patients. You will be asked to explain your educational and professional backgrounds, training and so on.

Tell the jury you cared about this patient and that you feel terrible about what occurred. But also let the jury know you treated the patient properly, that the injury happened despite your proper treatment and that you were not responsible for any injuries. Avoid all sarcasm and negativity.

After your attorney is finished with direct examination, the plaintiff's attorney will cross-examine you. This is the most difficult part of the case for you. Be calm and pleasant no matter what happens. Do not let yourself get angry. Remain caring, courteous and humble.

- Answer the questions you are asked truthfully and sincerely but do not volunteer information. Look the jurors in the eye. Do not let your anger overwhelm you. The plaintiff's attorney may get melodramatic, looking for ways to discredit you and blow things out of proportion. Do not forget that the plaintiff's attorney has a lot at stake here financially. The attorney will get one-third to one-half of any recovery plus costs, and if the plaintiff loses, plaintiff's attorney gets nothing. Do not give the attorney for the plaintiff the opportunity to bring out the worst in you.

- Plaintiff's counsel will then make a "Closing Argument," summarizing the facts presented during the trial and asking for an award in the plaintiff's favor.
- Defense counsel will then respond with a similar closing argument, summarizing the facts presented by the defense witnesses and disproving plaintiff's counsel's theories. Your attorney's goal is for the jury to conclude that the plaintiff's attorney did not meet the burden of proving the malpractice that was alleged.
- Jury deliberations occur next, during which time the jury members debate how to decide the case.
- Depending on the outcome, either or both of the parties may choose to appeal the case or file post-verdict motions.

Private Payment of Money

Doctors who want to avoid having their names in the Data Bank are allowed to pay out of pocket for any malpractice verdict. A later reimbursement from the insurance company is not sufficient – it has to be just your money. You will still have to disclose the settlement on all licensing, credentialing and other paperwork when asked about lawsuits. Settling a lawsuit with a "confidentiality" agreement but paying with the insurer's money will not help because the law relating to the Data Bank supersedes any private agreements to the contrary.

If you do pay, your attorney will prepare a "general release," for plaintiff to sign, releasing you from any and all liability to that patient arising from the incident. This document prevents the plaintiff from suing you again for the same injury.

Why Settle When You Did Nothing Wrong?

There are a number of reasons to simply settle a case:

- The emotional component. Being part of a medical malpractice suit takes a great toll on you as a doctor and as a person. The case often takes years to come to a conclusion. Few life experiences can stress you out as much for such a long period of time.
- The loss of income and personal life during the long hours preparing for the case and the long hours in the courtroom for a trial that can last several weeks.
- The fickleness of juries in general.
- The bad publicity that can result if you lose.

Yes, these are good reasons to settle sometimes even when you honestly and sincerely believe you are not at fault.

Forced Settlements

With the high cost of malpractice verdicts these days, insurance companies are tending to "force" settlements, because settlements do limit the amount of money expended by the carrier. The problem becomes, "Who is the client?" While the carrier is paying the patient, it is the doctor who ends up in the Data Bank. The potential conflict is easy to see, with the doctor wanting to defend himself or herself, and the insurance company wanting to cut its losses.

Verdicts

The size of the verdicts that juries have granted to plaintiffs injured by physicians can make a reasonable person cringe. Some awards are based on the fact that a bad injury occurred, even though the defendant doctor seemingly did nothing wrong. The reality is that doctors cannot perform miracles. Sometimes bad things do happen to good people. Some of the problems inherent in the jury system as it presently exists involve the fact that juries are required to hear cases regardless of the degree of special knowledge or expertise actually required to fully understand the issues. Therefore, juries hear complex cases, with no education or particular training.

Lawsuit Paperwork

After the lawsuit is finished, the original patient file should be replaced in your own patient file. Retain copies of the pleadings and the documents that ended the lawsuit. This way, you will be able to answer questions after when posed by your future malpractice carriers, the Data Bank, licensing agencies, et cetera.

Coping with Lawsuits

Most doctors who are sued for malpractice do not seek professional help afterwards, although studies do show that physicians who are sued suffer overwhelming stress in their personal and professional lives. The lawsuit is an affront to their personas, and they probably need professional therapy to deal with their anxiety, depression and other problems resulting from the litigation.

The emotional issues last for months and even years after the lawsuit ends. You may start "second guessing" yourself with patients, being less decisive, ordering more tests and additional consults, scheduling more follow-up visits and documenting charts more often. Coping with being sued is not easy.

Groundless Lawsuits… What Can You Do?

After you win, then what? You can sue back! Most such "countersuits" are brought by doctors alleging their patient's "wrongful use of civil process" or "malicious prosecution," which means having been sued improperly. In most states, a physician cannot file the countersuit until the original lawsuit is dismissed or the doctor has won after a trial.

Your odds of winning a countersuit are not great. It takes money and a lot of time to fight groundless lawsuits. It is often hard to find an attorney. You will have to personally pay attorney fees and all expenses. You usually have to pay an attorney hourly so be prepared to put your money where your mouth is. Even if you do win, you often do not win enough money to make the financial and emotional cost of suing worth the battle. Yes, it is tempting – but no, it is usually just not worth it.

Cures for the Malpractice Crisis

Although it is highly unlikely that the current medical malpractice situation will end any time in the near future, there are many suggestions being made about potential cures:

- To limit payment of non-economic damages in medical malpractice cases to a set sum, regardless of the extent of actual injury and regardless of the future expenses that will have to be paid over the patient's lifetime as a result of the medical error. This is a particularly unfair choice, because unfortunately, sometimes members of our profession do sometimes cause patients horrific injuries, and those patients deserve their just recompense.

- Putting a "cap" or limit on punitive damages, which serve to punish the wrongdoing rather than compensate injury. However, damages to punish the defendant are usually only awarded in really "outrageous" cases, not in the run-of-the-mill malpractice case.

- Requiring plaintiffs undergoing surgical procedures to purchase personal insurance coverage, which would pay them if injuries result. But patients are already paying for health insurance and copays – why should they pay more?

- Pretreatment arbitration agreements, where the parties decide in advance to accept an arbitrator's decision as binding. Instead of a judge or jury hearing the facts and the judge deciding the law on a particular issue, an arbitrator is used as the decision-maker. The arbitrator is generally independent, well trained and knowledgeable in the medical field. Because this person is neutral, both sides generally better accept the decision. ADR is a fast, simple and relatively inexpensive way to have a decision made in a health care scenario.

- Another rational suggestion is that all medical malpractice claims be handled by doctor/lawyer panels who are educated in the medical and legal issues, and who are competent to understand the complex fact patterns that medical malpractice cases often weave.

Chapter 5: Data Banks

"Disclosure" and "accountability" are the catchwords of medicine in the 21st century. There are a number of different reporting agencies that seek to hold doctors accountable to the public.

National Practitioner Data Bank

The Health Care Quality Improvement Act of 1986 established the National Practitioner Data Bank. The Data Bank was created to improve the quality of health care by encouraging all hospitals, state licensing boards and other health care facilities to name and discipline those who engage in unprofessional conduct. Another goal was to restrict incompetent doctors and other health care professionals from moving state to state without disclosing the sins of their past.

In an effort to provide relevant information about a health care practitioner's professional credentials, the Data Bank maintains information about various aspects of a doctor's professional life:

- Information relating to payments to plaintiffs injured in medical malpractice cases, including names of doctors and hospitals against whom a settlement or verdict has been reached.

- Records of certain discipline and sanctions taken against doctors, including adverse actions against physicians involving their licenses, clinical privileges and professional society memberships, as well as all rejections, restrictions and terminations of privileges and hospital disciplinary restrictions of 30 days or more.
- All adverse actions from peer review committees.

When information is included in the Data Bank, you are given the right to briefly explain your "side," and this written explanation is appended to your Data Bank file if you wish.

Accessibility of the Information: Generally, the information contained in the Data Bank may only be accessed by:

- State licensing boards
- Health care facilities
- The affected physician.

The general public may access only general information that does not identify any particular entity or practitioner. Because the information is totally confidential, if a disclosure violation occurs, the wrongdoer may have to pay penalties.

Personal payments are excluded: If you pay for a medical malpractice settlement out of your personal funds, as long as you are never reimbursed for that payment by your insurer, then your name will be protected and you will not be "entered" into the Data Bank. If your practice pays the settlement amount, the practice's name will be sent to the Data Bank instead.

If you do pay privately so as to keep your name out of the Data Bank, you still must disclose the underlying circumstances when asked about prior lawsuits, et cetera on applications for staff privileges, malpractice insurance applications and the like.

National Healthcare and Protection Data Bank

In an effort to fight fraud and abuse in health insurance and health care delivery, the Healthcare Integrity and Protection Data Bank (HIPDB) was established by the Health Insurance Portability and Accountability Act of 1996. Reporting to the data bank started in November, 1999. The information maintained by HIPDB overlaps to some extent the information contained in the National Practitioners Data

Bank. HIPDB information requires that all state and federal enforcement organizations furnish information to it concerning:

- Civil judgments
- Criminal convictions and
- Actions by any licensing agencies against a health care provider, supplier or practitioner related to the delivery of a health care item or service.

Access to the HIPDB data is restricted in a manner similar to the National Practitioner Data Bank.

State Information Repositories

Some states are implementing Websites that let the public discover any disciplinary actions against you. In Pennsylvania, for example, a doctor can verify information about his or her own license status, and the general public can learn about disciplinary matters, from a state website. Other information is also available from sites such as the American Medical Association's Doctor Finder site.

In addition to the above, the Center for Medicare and Medicaid Services (CMS, formerly HCFA), releases quarterly "report card" of sorts for each Medicare provider, publishing numerical scores for various stated criteria.

Information about being excluded from participating in federal health care programs can be found at https://oig.hhs.gov/exclusions/background.asp. You can also check to see if any particular physician is excluded.

Check Your Status

Check your status in the various sites to ensure accuracy.

Conclusion

I have given you a general overview of the types of medical malpractice insurance required to practice medicine in most states in addition to a background so that you may formulate ideas on how to avoid lawsuits in medicine. This should make you aware of the types of lawsuits that can occur with the practice of medicine and how to potentially avoid them. I also generally outlined the stages of a medical malpractice lawsuit should one occur.

No healthcare professional intends to have a bad outcome when caring for patients. Medicine is not an exact science. There is an "art" to medicine and taking care of patients. Each patient you care for is unique and as such, there is always the potential for something to go wrong. This occurs despite having the best systems for risk prevention in place and your best intent otherwise. This book will give you the basic understanding you need with regard to the medical malpractice arena to help you do your best job and make you aware of the medical-legal system in which we live.

I wish you the best of luck with your professional endeavors.

MedLaw Compliance Inquiry Form

Fill out this form to stay in touch, schedule a strategy session with Dr. Moses or a Team Member to request a complimentary strategy session.

Your Name: _____

Your Title: _____

Business Name: _____

Mobile Phone: _____

Direct Email: _____

Website: _____

What do you want to discuss with Dr. Moses or his team?

- ☐ **FOLLOW UP WITH ME** during or after the event.
- ☐ **Educational Programs:** Both online and on-site for healthcare providers, insurance industry professionals, administrators, student physicians, and Board members.
- ☐ **Speaking Engagements:** On current and future risk issues on preventing medical malpractice and

compliance violations, the changing healthcare reimbursement system from fee-for-service to value-based, burnout, and the general state of the practice of Medicine.

☐ **Consulting:** including reviews of filed medical malpractice cases or potential malpractice cases for defensibility and quality of medicine for defensibility, areas of risk, and compliance.

☐ Other: _____

_____

Please Attach Your Business Card to this Form or logon to:
http://www.medlawcompliance.com/contact-us

About

Richard E. Moses, D.O., J.D., F.C.L.M.

Richard E. Moses has practiced Gastroenterology and Hepatology in the Philadelphia, Pennsylvania area since 1984. He is board certified in Internal Medicine, Gastroenterology, and Forensic Medicine. An Adjunct Clinical Professor of Medicine at the Temple University School of Medicine, he holds numerous administrative and consultative positions with state and national medical societies, and has held numerous leadership positions on committees for various hospital staffs throughout his years of medical practice.

He is the Chairman of the Department of Medicine, and Associate Medical Director for Medical Staff Development and Relations at Jeanes Hospital, part of the Temple University Health Care System, actively recruiting and developing physician practices and integrating healthcare relationships and services.

Dr. Moses is additionally an attorney, having graduated from the Temple University School of Law in 1997. He has been an Adjunct Professor of Law there since his graduation, teaching a course entitled "Current Problems in Law and Medicine." He lectures for Health Law classes and at medical, legal, compliance conferences, and health care institutions on a variety of medical-legal topics.

Richard provides risk management and educational consulting in the areas of patient safety, medical professional liability, health care compliance, the state of the changing health care system, medical provider well-being, and medical ethics. A national speaker and author of books, numerous articles and book chapters, he routinely functions as an adviser and program director for medical, legal, risk management and compliance issues, in addition to authoring and editing accredited programs on these topics.

He can be reached at: www.MedLawCompliance.com.

Engaging Dr. Moses to Speak

Book Dr. Moses as Your Keynote Speaker and You Are Guaranteed to Make Your Event Inspirational, Motivational, Educational, Highly Entertaining and Unforgettable!

For over three decades, Dr. Moses has been educating, entertaining, motivating and inspiring:

- Physicians
- Physician Assistants
- Nurse Practitioners
- Other Advanced Practice Providers
- Physicians in training programs
- Compliance Officers and personnel
- Healthcare employees including nurses
- Healthcare executives and leaders
- Health Systems
- Local and National Medical and Legal Organizations
- Medical Insurance Companies
- Compliance Officers and Compliance Departments

about medical, legal, risk management and compliance issues and strategies.

While maintaining a busy active private medical practice caring for and advocating for his patients, Dr. Moses is in the minority of physicians having a law degree who actively teaches at a law school and medical school level.

Dr. Moses is also actively involved with state and national medical societies following the legislative trends that are initiating change and addressing future challenges.

Additionally, he consults with healthcare leaders and healthcare system administrators as a result of his multifaceted background and talents.

This rare combination has given him unsurpassed expertise and insight such that he is considered a visionary in the medical-legal ramifications of our evolving healthcare system. Dr. Moses has the uncanny ability to understand and educate virtually everyone on medical, legal, ethical, and compliance issues that create risk for patients, healthcare systems, medical malpractice insurance companies and physicians at all levels of their career.

For more information and to book Dr. Moses for your next event, visit www.MedLawCompliance.com/Contact-Us

CPSIA information can be obtained
at www.ICGtesting.com
Printed in the USA
BVHW040208081121
621066BV00015B/670

9 781981 803415